HIDDEN TREASURES

HALIFAX

Edited by Chris Hallam

First published in Great Britain in 2002 by
YOUNG WRITERS
Remus House,
Coltsfoot Drive,
Peterborough, PE2 9JX
Telephone (01733) 890066

HB ISBN 0 75434 040 6
SB ISBN 0 75434 041 4

FOREWORD

This year, the Young Writers' Hidden Treasures competition proudly presents a showcase of the best poetic talent from over 72,000 up-and-coming writers nationwide.

Young Writers was established in 1991 and we are still successful, even in today's technologically-led world, in promoting and encouraging the reading and writing of poetry.

The thought, effort, imagination and hard work put into each poem impressed us all, and once again, the task of selecting poems was a difficult one, but nevertheless, an enjoyable experience.

We hope you are as pleased as we are with the final selection and that you and your family continue to be entertained with *Hidden Treasures Halifax* for many years to come.

CONTENTS

David Watkin	68
Lorna Butler	69
Matthew Walton	70
Arabella Fox	71
David Wevill	72
Jenny Wormald	73
William Edhouse	74
Ben Taylor	75

Luddenden Dene J&I School

Louis Sheridan	76
Claire Kneeshaw	77
Charlotte Gross	78
Nicola Walker	79
Ryan Barrett	80
Hannah Walker	81
Leon Wadsworth	82
Billy Painter	83
Natalie Hirst	84
Thomas Lund	85
Bethany Broadbent	86
Sadie Parkin	87
Gemma Greenberry	88
Edward Whiteley	89
Lisa Wehden	90
Jon Galloway	91
Aaron John Alexander	92

Northowram J&I School

Jordan Haley	93
Danielle Graham	94
Lydia Gibson	95
Emily Godfrey	96
Toby Greenhough	97
Rebecca Kitson	98
Robin Dance	99
Brittany Henderson	100
Ben Glennon	101

Joshua Magro	177
Samantha Egan	178
Christopher Turver	179
Kirsty O'Halloran	180
Bradley Holroyd	181

Salterlee Primary School

Emily Horton	182
Hannah Bodrozic	183
Charlotte Lines	184
Daniel Greenwood	185
Freya Thoseby	186
Francesca Bland	187
Amy Duckett	188
Christian Georgiou	189
Niall Smith	190
Danielle Stephenson	191
Danielle Cotton	192
Natasha O'Hara	193
Calum Smith	194

Wainstalls J&I School

Isobel Mears-Sykes	195
Lynsie Link	196
Holly Beaumont	197
Joshua Ward	198
Daniel Futerko	199
Stacey Link	200
Sophie Smith	201
Olivia Sutcliffe	202
Jess Lumb	203
Sophie Hoyle	204
Thomas Thorp	205
Xavier St Hilaire-Knowles	206
Gemma Dyson	207
Ben Wilby	208
Natalie Carter	209
Hannah Moran	210

The Poems

TREASURE

Treasure can be anything
From coins to diamond rings
Rubies, pearls and emeralds
And lots of other things
Whether in the sand
Or deep below the sea
If you find any treasure
Then it belongs to me!

Alaïs Ricard (10)
Boston Spa CE School

HIDDEN TREASURE

Round and round the labyrinth
To the sparkling gold.
Some rooms round, some rooms square,
Creatures lurking here and there.

Monsters big, monsters small
All in the shape of warty dragons.
Red, green and black,
With maliciously glinting eyes,
Creeping round the passages in deep black darkness.

Passages winding this way and that
Here, there, everywhere.
Left, right; right, left,
At every fork a constant fight of which way to go,
Left or right?

Finally in the middle is the gold,
All shiny and glittering in the darkness.
Quickly I stash it in my pockets and run back through
The toilsome, tiresome, troublesome maze,
Back into the daylight
Where the gold shimmers like the sun.

Liam Livesley (8)
Boston Spa CE School

BRITAIN

Bold and courageous soldiers
Risking their lives for us
I don't know about you but I'm grateful.
They should be knighted.
A load of heroes
In our lives, they
Never give up and neither should we.

Lucie Grainger (10)
Boston Spa CE School

PIRATES' BALL

Turn the wheel
toot the horn
pull up the flag
we are having a ball.

With flashing lights
and lemonade
all the food
of a pirate's age.

Natalie Heaton (8)
Boston Spa CE School

THE UNDERWATER CAVE

In the bottom of the deep blue sea,
There was a man who never swam.
His name was Mr Blobby
He was usually known as Robbie.

The forbidden cave was haunted,
By taunted voices.
The noise was bugging Robbie,
As he was swimming through the lobby.

He hated the voices,
He had one of two choices.
To go, or, to stay, out of harms way.

He decided to go,
To find his foe
And then battle it till the end of its time.

Sam Benn (8)
Boston Spa CE School

You're

You're my sweetie-pie
You're like the scent of a flower.
You're the god,
You're nowhere near a lemon so sour.

You're the one so high,
You're like a cute bunny.
You're the best in the world,
You're my favourite.

You're the treasure,
You're my best friend.
You're nice and cosy
Who doesn't drive me round the bend.

You're my mum!

Luke Foulds (8)
Bowling Green J&I School

FOR MY TEACHER

In the morning
When I come in to school
I see my teacher.

She smiles like the sunset
And dresses like a pop star
She smells like berries.

When I pick my pen up
I just want to write
About all the super things
My teacher really does.

Kealy Holroyd (9)
Bowling Green J&I School

LEGO TOYS!

Bits and bobs,
And cats and dogs.
They're cute and furry and soft and cuddly.
They're fun to play with,
And great for pets.
But the best thing is you're the best.

Jack Baxendale (9)
Bowling Green J&I School

YOU'RE SIMPLY THE BEST

You're the teddy bear
I cuddle up with at night.
You're the lovely smell of fresh baked bread
I eat in the morning.
You're the bright sun rays
That shine down on me.
You're the warm hot chocolate
I have on a winter's day.
You're the hot bubble bath
When I am all chilly.
You're the cool glass of water
When I am boiling hot.
You're simply the best and I love you.

Alexandra Avis (9)
Bowling Green J&I School

THE GOO!

In the morning after school, I smell goo
It's in the biggest pan too
It bubbles up and round
Squeaks and makes a nasty sound.

Eyeballs and mice,
Kites and lights
Ants crawl on top
To make it more like rock!

Enrico Bissolati (9)
Bowling Green J&I School

THE ODD OLD HOUSE

I'm walking through the forest
I see an old house.
I feel kind of scared
I feel like going home.
It looks kind of nice.
The flowers are pink
Yellow and green.
They don't sound mean.

I walk up the path
I feel kind of lost.
I feel like I'm on a raft.
I knock on the door.
A lady opened the door.
She's very, very tall
She'd just been to the Mall.
She said 'Come in with me
And I'll give you some tea.'

Tom Ingham (9)
Bowling Green J&I School

YOU'RE

You're as sweet as candyfloss, as warm as hot chocolate.
You make me happy whenever you're around.
You smell as clean as a freshly made bed and when
You're in a really good mood you smell like
A really beautiful smelling freshly opened bag of chocolate eclairs.
When you give me hugs they keep me warm for hours on end.
You're always giving me money
The toys you buy me I play with for hours and hours
All these things remind me of you!

Ella Tidswell (9)
Bowling Green J&I School

WHEN I WAS YOUNG

When I was young
I used to say
'What shall we play?'
and
'What a day!'

We played rugby
And on the rugby pitch
There was a ditch
I fell on the pitch
And went down the ditch
How did I get to be old?

Jordan Steele (9)
Bowling Green J&I School

MY POTION!

In goes the marmalade, butter and sugar
In goes the toothpaste, water and milk
In goes the rabbit food, carrots and peas
In goes the brandy, whisky and port.

Now Mum and Dad are home
And Mum asks for a coffee
I'm so fed up with it so in goes my potion.

Mum drank the coffee
Then she went to bed
Now she's got a headache
Now she's been sick
I really shouldn't have done that.

Mum and Dad went shopping,
So they were gone all day
Then out comes the saucepan
And the mixer too.

In goes the vinegar, chips and mushy peas,
In goes the ink, cold soup and mustard
In goes the red wine, white wine and custard
In goes the beer, geese food and soap.

Dad wants a coffee
So in goes my potion
Dad drank his coffee
Then he went to bed
I really shouldn't have done that.

Katie Dyson (9)
Bowling Green J&I School

THE BEACH

I love the soft breeze at the beach
And the sunbathing on the sand
I love the people talking aloud
And sometimes the noisy band.

I love the children making sandcastles
And playing in the sea
I love the sunbed as I fall asleep
And the nice warm cup of tea.

It's sometimes nice to have a swim
Or feel the warm silk sand
I like to talk to friends of mine
And smell people's wet hands.

When I get home
I unpack my bags
It's chilly back here
I'd better get my warm glad rags!

Rachel Whalley (9)
Bowling Green J&I School

FRIENDS FOREVER

You're cuddly and soft
You make me laugh and cry
You're like a furry Furby
You're my friends because we like each other
We're best friends.

You eat pizza, candyfloss and ice cream
You're like my rabbit and guinea pig
You have dogs, I like them
You think my mum is pretty
You're my friends, best friends.

Bethany Fallon (9)
Bowling Green J&I School

YOU'RE

You're my wizard to sort anything
When you think.
You're my bubbling potion.
You're my rushing blizzard.
When I need you
When I run past you.
You're like a waft of lotion.

You're like my PlayStation
Because you play with me.
You're my championship motor cross
Like a mud bike loud and fast.
You're my mint model builder.
You're my cruise ship
To take me places.

But you're the best, my everything.

Matthew Noble (9)
Bowling Green J&I School

YOU'RE ALL THE SEASONS

You're my summer mornings bright
You're my winter fire alight
You're the sensational flowers in spring
You're the autumn leaves floating and dancing.

You're the blazing sun in summer
You're the freezing snow in winter
You're the beautiful butterflies in spring
You're the leaves in autumn like golden rings
You're all the seasons long and short
You're my favourite thing of all.

Emma Weeden (9)
Bowling Green J&I School

My Bike

I like the green on your frame
I see your cogs turning around
I see your wheels zooming ahead
Then your brakes tightening to slow me down.

I smell your oil in your cogs
I smell the rust coming from your frame
I smell the rubber when I do my skids
As I ride I shout my name.

I touch the brakes when I can't stop
I touch the pedals when I want to go faster
I touch the seat when I'm doing stunts
And when I fall off it is a disaster!

Frederick Walker (9)
Bowling Green J&I School

TEDDIES

My cute and cuddly teddies
Their soft, silky, fluffy fur
Keeps me warm at night.

When I get lonely
You're my company
When I get scared
You're the one who comforts me
And looks as bright as light.

I like huge and tiny teddies
They're all really nice
They get me through the night.

Danielle Norcliffe (9)
Bowling Green J&I School

STARS

Stars so sparkly bright
in the light of the moon.
They are so beautiful
they make me feel shiny.

They make me feel
merry, cheerful and sunny.
Every time I go to bed I look at
the stars and wonder.

Stars are so
brilliant because
they are so twinkly.
They give me a warm feeling before
I go to bed.

Rebecca Holdsworth (8)
Bowling Green J&I School

THE FOOTBALL MATCH

At Mrs Hibbert's house
If you want to make a smell
She will ring a bell
I went to a football match
There was a great black patch
I thought I saw a witch
My mum said it was jiggery pokery
After all that excitement
I looked at my watch
It was time for butterscotch!

Sean Morrow (8)
Bowling Green J&I School

YOU

You are the one who looked after me
You were the one who told me to beware
You were the one who taught me how to climb a tree
And you were the one who told me not to stare.

You were the one to tell me to ride
You were the one who gave me pride
You were the one who puts me to bed
And you are the one who made me love you.

Francesca Jones (9)
Bowling Green J&I School

IN THE WOODS

On a Sunday afternoon when I walk into the woods
I hear the birds singing sweetly as the squirrels scatter their nuts.
I love the smell of flowers in the spring.
Sometimes I hear the church bells ring.

I like to hear people laughing.
I love the woods because it makes me happy as a lark.
I like to lie in the long green grass
And watch the white, white clouds go by.

Robyn Ward (8)
Holywell Green Primary School

AT THE VILLAGE

When I'm in the village I can see birds in the bright blue sky
I can hear people singing all around me
When I'm in the village I can hear birds chirping in the blue sky.

I can smell fresh baked bread
When I'm in the village I can see colourful flags
and colourful ribbons on the maypole.
I can see people sitting in the shade.

Lisa Atter (8)
Holywell Green Primary School

IN THE CITY

In the city
I love the smell of KFC
wafting up my nostrils
I can hear the shouting
of the greengrocer and
the ringing of the phones
as I walk up the market.

In the marketplace
there's a fresh meat
stall that sells delicious
meats and a lovely floating
smell of pork drifting
up my nose as I head
home with my mouth watering.

In the town
I love the smell of cheeseburgers
floating up my nose I can hear the
cars revving and the ringing of the church bell
shouting 'Come here now thief.'
I see people trying
To get out of their
flats and shops
I see objects being
robbed in broad
daylight.

Sam Harris (9)
Holywell Green Primary School

THE SEASIDE

I can see the swimming pool far away
The busy streets blocking my way
The golden trees shining like the rays of sun
I like the smell of fish and chips
I like the sound of the sea crashing against the rocks
Shops selling sweets and rock that I like
When I wake up in the morning the view is beautiful
I walk around the block every morning
When I walk past the school, I hear the school bell ringing.

Victoria Charity (8)
Holywell Green Primary School

IN THE COUNTRYSIDE

I can see the birds flying around the barn
I can hear the tractor driving along the lane
I can feel the grass tickling my toes
I can see the clouds shaped like cars in the sky
I can hear horses galloping over the meadows
I love the sights and sounds of the countryside,
Drifting to my eyes and ears.

Christopher Schofield (9)
Holywell Green Primary School

AT THE SWIMMING POOL

Every Saturday morning
I go to the swimming pool.
I hear the sound of laughter and
People splashing everyone.
They turn on the wave machine and
I float along the water having great fun.

The swimming pool is crowded
So I bang into people.
They shout and scream so
I swim past.
When I'm swimming
I see babies in rubber rings playing with their mums.

When I swim I get dunked under
And the chlorine hurts my eyes.
I swallow it, it makes me feel sick
I go under the fountain and get really wet.

I see people diving in the
Sparkling water.
But I have to go home, my
Colour has been called out.
I go to the sweet machine
And get some sweets.

Funmi Alaiyemola (8)
Holywell Green Primary School

THE SUMMER WIND

The summer wind is soft and breezy
The summer wind is warm and calm
The summer wind is refreshing
The summer wind is fresh.

The summer wind is cooling
The summer wind is smooth
The summer wind is warm and silent
In the summer you will feel the summer wind
Wafting through your hair.

Toni Dyson-Howley (9)
Holywell Green Primary School

WATCH OUT FOR THE WINTER WIND

The icy winter wind can blow you away
on an incredibly windy day. Well
I used to know a man called Mark
but he got swept right through the park
and he couldn't move until it was dark!
So . . . watch out for the winter wind.

The winter wind is extremely strong
it can even stop you while moving along.
I knew a princess called Alice
and she couldn't get away from her palace,
so she got a drink and lost her chalice.
So . . . watch out for, watch out for,
Watch out for the winter wind!

Daniel Nolan (9)
Holywell Green Primary School

FISH

Down, down in the sea
me and my friend and my
dog called Lee.
We are going fishing today.
Little fish, big fish, stripy fish,
spotty fish, red fish, dead fish
oh no, *shark!*
Quick it's getting dark.
Row fast.
Phew, we're at the shore at last.

William Berrett (8)
Holywell Green Primary School

WHEN I'M SWIMMING

I can smell chlorine drifting up my nose.
I can float lightly in a ring.

I like to dive in the water
And spring up and down.

I feel happy and joyful
I like to whizz down a waterslide, as long as Daddy's by my side.

Hollie Gregory (8)
Holywell Green Primary School

SUMMER WIND

The summer wind
calls my name in the breeze.

The summer wind
does not blow me down.

The summer wind
is refreshing in the summer air.

I get up in the morning
the sun is in my room.

The bride is at the church in the summer wind
waiting for the groom.

The wind is smooth and sweet
as I play outside
the summer wind is soft and gentle.

Laura Young (9)
Holywell Green Primary School

ON THE BEACH

The silky golden sand you can build sandcastles out of it.
You can walk in it with your bare feet.

Sunbathe on the sand.
Swim in the sea, find shells on the beach.

I like the salty sand and shiny sun, it makes me want to sunbathe.
You can climb the rocks that go around the beach.

Luke Attiwell (8)
Holywell Green Primary School

THE SUMMER WIND

The summer wind
is warm and gentle.

It smells like a
beautiful flower.

It blows along
the streets and
makes people
happy.

Sometimes it is
mischievous
because it blows
petals off the
flowers.

Daniel Mitchell (9)
Holywell Green Primary School

IN THE STREETS

I love the smell of fish and chips.
My nose sniffing beautiful curry to dip my chips in.
You go to the café and get a gorgeous piece of lemon cake
                              covered with lemon icing.

Go to the bakery and smell the freshly baked bread and ginger, *umm!*

People talking in the streets, nobody's ever going to get any peace.

Gary Barnes (8)
Holywell Green Primary School

I Love The Harbour

I love the harbour with all the wonderful boats bobbing up and down.
I love to hear the birds singing sweetly.
What about the sea, swaying side to side.
I love the smell of salt drifting up my nose.

I love the beautiful view of the bushy trees and rocky mountains
in the distance, and big buildings above the sea.
It is wonderful!

Antony Brown (9)
Holywell Green Primary School

DAYS OF THE WEEK

On Saturday morning I smell the wondrous smell of the baker'shop.
I could taste the glorious taste of an iced bun,
with a juicy cherry on the top,
and as it was bought for me I get wondrously happy.

On Sunday I am at my dad's
I sit and watch TV
Then I smell the glorious smell of the fish and chip shop
Then I know I'll want fish and chips for my dinner.

On Monday night I go to Brownies to play games and have fun
I enjoy going to Brownies but when I have to go home it's sad.

On Tuesday I go to French to learn French
because each year I go to France.

On Wednesday I go to netball, I really enjoy it,
it's a really good game.

On Thursday I watch Buffy the Vampire Slayer,
sometimes it's really scary.

On Friday I watch the new series of Buffy and Angel,
which is the best thing ever.

Deborah Kerr (9)
Holywell Green Primary School

THE MIRACLE BOX

In my box I will put a flame from a dragon with its tail alight.
The shimmer of a crystal dress.
A flash from a thunderbird flying across the ocean.
A glittering reindeer soaring to the North Pole.
A blast of water from a turtle with two spouts floating across the river.

Jay Govindji (9)
Lightcliffe Preparatory School

IN MY MAGIC BOX

A dinosaur with a helmet with a blasting blade.
The first three wishes from an ugly genie.
The silky webs made by a glowing spider.
The spark from a magnificent electric fish.

Adam Heley (8)
Lightcliffe Preparatory School

THE MAGIC BOX

I will put in the box
A sparkling feather of a snow white swan swimming in an
azure blue lake.
A jar of singing musical voices
And a ball of invisible string.

My magic box is made from glistening snowflakes and
crimson mahogany engraved in silver metal.

I will put in the box
The tiniest grain of sand from a sun yellow beach
The glint of gold from a heavenly angel's halo
And a lunatic in one of the last green bottles hanging on the wall.

Natasha North (8)
Lightcliffe Preparatory School

THE MERMAID'S BOX

In my magic box I will put
The sound of a falling leaf off an autumn tree.
A drop of icy water from the sparkling winter river.
A tiny piece of Santa's glinting caring magic.
The swishy wag of a puppy dog's tail.
The click of the smallest key opening a rickety dungeon door.
My box is old fashioned, made from bits of the moon and sun.
A strong language is engraved in gold on the lid.

Talia Gianotti (9)
Lightcliffe Preparatory School

THE ZEBRA BOX

I will put in my box
Brightest blossom petals from the summer tree
Swishes of colourful leaves swirling in a bluffer of spring
A flickering flame from the blazing sun
A quack from a silly, silver, barking duck
The whitest rabbits tail with a sparkling crystal on the end.

My box is made out of silver and gold flowers with secret pockets in
each side and its corners are made of zebra's feet.

Laura Wood (8)
Lightcliffe Preparatory School

THE MAGIC BOX

I will put in my box
A twitch of the silver budgie's tail.
The first wave that hit the golden English beach.
The last jump of the one toothed whale of the Arctic.
The flap of the great white sharks fin.
The violet toe of the last T-rex.
My box is made out of Rudolph's antlers
The hinges are made out of frogs' legs.

Adam Greathead (8)
Lightcliffe Preparatory School

THE MAGIC BOX

In my magic box I will put
The hee-haw of a hungry donkey waiting for some grass.
The sparkle of a glass shoe that the prince is carrying on a cushion.
The snowy tip of a mountain.
The meaty smell of pork just coming out of the oven.
The slither of a snake's tongue.

My box is made of bronze and metal
Its hinges are made of jaw bones and
On the lid is the moon with sparkling stars around it.

Jack Hoyle (9)
Lightcliffe Preparatory School

THE SUN

Shines
like a beautiful crystal all over the world.

Bakes
like a chicken in a very hot over or a
piece of toast in a toaster.

Scorches
the world like it's an egg in a frying pan.

Burns
like a fantastic flaming fire on Bonfire Night.

Sparkles
very brightly every day when we all awaken.

Kirsty Narey (9)
Lightcliffe Preparatory School

THE MAGIC BOX

I will put in my box
A duck with a silver beak paddling in the sea
A fierce tiger with yellow spots
The howl of a hungry wolf from a faraway mountain
A hoot from a lost owl in a forest of wonder
A sparkle of silver treasure.

James Firth (8)
Lightcliffe Preparatory School

THE MAGIC BOX

I'm going to put a bark of a dark brown dog in the magic box
I will put in a roar of a live yellow bear in the box
A waterfall of one wish and a glass book of spells
I'm going to put a whizzing shooting golden star
I will put in a silver sparkling shining crystal.

Thomas Nicholson (9)
Lightcliffe Preparatory School

THE MAGICIAN'S BOX

In my magic box I will put . . .
The first brave wiggle of a scared weak puppy's tail
A tiny despairing drop of sea sail
The shine of the tender panda's glossy black coat
The sparkle of the diamond in the treasure clam
The ear-splitting shriek of the lamp of light
In the coldest darkest dungeon in the lost world

My box is made from golden snow
With ancient castles on the sides and rhinos on the top
My hinges are made of the hottest fire.

Jessica Crowther (9)
Lightcliffe Preparatory School

THE ENCHANTED BOX

In my enchanted box
I will put a magic horn from a snow-white unicorn.
The cream colour of a polar bear's breath.
The smell of a rose which has just burst open.
The swish of the first page in a legendary book being turned.
The last slurp of a sumptuous raspberry milkshake.
The slithery scale from a fierce, terrifying dragon who captured a
                                    glamorous princess in distress.

My box is made from cold blue ice,
Fashioned with fairies and snowflakes.
The hinges are joined with ancient golden writing.

Elizabeth Learoyd (9)
Lightcliffe Preparatory School

THE SUN

Warms
the world with a hot friendly glow.

Glitters
as an everlasting burning woman with fiery eyes.

Scorches
like the hottest fire that burns inside a heart of flames.

Shines
like a sparkling crystal that dazzles my eyes.

Is a ball
of ruby-red fire that the moon's children play with at night.

Gabrielle Cooke (8)
Lightcliffe Preparatory School

THE MAGIC BOX

In my box I will put
The fork of lightning that comes hurtling down to Earth.
The stamp of a foot that's squashing an ant.
A person from Mars that's jumping in space.
The last piece of the moon on a gold shooting star.
A sharp pointed tooth of a Siamese cat.

My box is made of a tooth of a dinosaur and a thunder cloud.

John Sugden (8)
Lightcliffe Preparatory School

MY HAMSTER LINFORD

My hamster Linford is fat and three years old.
He is brown and white with patches of black on him.
The cage is a penthouse.
In it he has a hamster igloo, play wheels and tunnels.
He dances to any music I put on,
Only if I hold him round the waist
His favourite food is carrots, boiled eggs, cabbage and peanuts.
He loves to roll about in his green play ball.
I think he is timid and shy.
Once he got lost under the bed.
The cats stare endlessly at him and he stares back.
His minute, pink hairy tail is beautiful.
He is so very cute.

James Chand Madan (10)
Lightcliffe Preparatory School

THE LONELY GIRL

The lonely little girl stands alone in the deserted street
She is bored and friendless
She hasn't got anybody to talk to
She is very, very unhappy and cheerless
She wishes she had a friend to play with
She is very timid and scared
She has a little face which looks ever so lonely
No one will play with her
The lonely little girl still stands alone in the deserted street.

Francesca Verity (10)
Lightcliffe Preparatory School

MY HAMSTER TOFFEE

My hamster Toffee has black eyes as black as coal
He loves to play all the day with his lime green ball.
When I have to go he always whimpers
But I tell him it's alright I'll be home.
He loves to see and play with his reflection.
Sometimes he escapes and we always get in a panic.
Then we cannot find him we look all over
But he's never there so we look outside.
Now the years have passed and he's escaped
We found him dead by the next-door neighbour's gate.
We don't know why but we think it is their cats.

Kathryn Bate (9)
Lightcliffe Preparatory School

ON THE MOORS

I live near the moor where the railway children used to live.
In the Three Chimney house.
Me and my Nana love to walk Barclay and Henry, they love it too.
I love it when the sun shines down on the long smooth grass.
I love it in the winter when we see the robin's ruby-red breast,
And its soft brown feathers.

It's beautiful up on the moors.

Ellie Waddington (9)
Lightcliffe Preparatory School

MY CAT JESS

My cat Jess is fast and silky
She always gets in the way
My cat Jess sleeps anywhere
She even sleeps on my back
She eats chicken and duck
In jelly of course
She has one white eye and one black one
She's furry and soft and gentle
But sometimes she bites me
My cat Jess does not like dogs.

Lyndon Ashley (9)
Lightcliffe Preparatory School

MAD MOGGY MOODS

You will find her in the chair doing
somersaults to get her tail.
When she sits in the window her body is as thin as a rake,
but I still love her.
In a morning she's crazy and wild,
on a night she's soft and cute,
but I still love her.
At the weekend she's fast and as
Mad as a March hare.
But after all she's my best friend
and I love her.

Rebecca Stobart (9)
Lightcliffe Preparatory School

MY PONY MATE MONTY!

Monty just loves jumping
I wish he was mine.
He's my uncle Andrew's pony though
but I wish he was mine.
Once we've been out riding he's a big slobber chops
but still I wish he was mine.
My uncle Andrew got him from a riding school
but every day
I think or say
I wish he was mine!
My 'Mr Mont' he's a famous showjumper's son
I wish he was mine.
Every summer he rubs and rubs so his mane is quite short
but still I wish he was mine.

Sarah Wevill (9)
Lightcliffe Preparatory School

THE HILLS AND FIELDS

The hills and fields are beautiful and green
The grass is really cosy
I like to roll around on the fields
The hills are hard to climb
But sometimes me and my gran think it's fine
I like it when the sun is shining
It shines down like a ball of fire
The hills and fields are nice and bright
When me and Gran take the dog with us he rolls around too!

Philippa Gledhill (9)
Lightcliffe Preparatory School

MY HAMSTER SUE

My hamster Sue is as golden as the sun
She has black splodges
She is always getting lost
And can get through any gaps
She has a little pink nose as though it was a tiny peach
The same with her paws, but with little tiny claws
Her beady eyes are always looking behind her to see if the cat is there
Sue is my hamster and when she dies I will miss her.

Rebecca Sutton (10)
Lightcliffe Preparatory School

THE BIG MATCH LIVE

We wait for the whistle
While we eat our burgers and chips.
We sing and cheer like thirty grizzly bears.
They come on to the pitch and we
Throw balloons all over the ground.
He blows his whistle and it starts.
They have a chance but Nigel saves it
And at the other end there's a fight.
He blows his whistle for half time
It starts again. Fowler shoots and
Scores and we run onto the pitch.
We go back to our seats and
When we sit down they score.
He blows his whistle it's the end
And we go back really happy.

William Hatfield (10)
Lightcliffe Preparatory School

MY PETS

My dog is a smelly old log that eats like a hog.
My cat is an annoying old rat that thinks is a bat.
My bird is an ill-mannered nerd, very dumb and says bad words.
But my family is very fun and not at the least bit dumb
But I love my pets and my family and that's what matters.

Luke Thompson (9)
Lightcliffe Preparatory School

HAMSTER

My hamster died
It got fried in a chip pan
It passed away that day
My dad said to get a new one
That day I sat on a staircase gazing into thin air
It was so unfair
I couldn't get to sleep that night
It was as if I had lost a fight.

Joshua Thompson (10)
Lightcliffe Preparatory School

MY DOGS

My dogs are always chewing logs
My dogs always fight
My dogs always bite
My dogs always growl
The dogs always prowl
My dogs always bark
They love to walk in the park
My dogs share their toys
After all boys will be boys.

Richard O'Hara (9)
Lightcliffe Preparatory School

FAT FRED

Fat Fred eats all the things that are bad for you.
Fat Fred's favourite foods are all the rich things like
treacle, chocolate and tarts.
Fat Fred's mum Freda goes shopping every week for him
because he is so fat.
Fat Fred doesn't have a dad
He died of a heart attack.
Fat Fred is as tall as a treacle jar and he is as fat as a motor car.

Ben Sutton (10)
Lightcliffe Preparatory School

MY DOG JACK

My dog Jack is a Labrador, he's cute, funny, noisy and loves to dig.
He always gets in the way though but we still love him.
I'm always kind and always give him chicken
But my mum always tells me off for giving him that.
My dog Jack loves long walks although he doesn't walk fast
he always makes it fun.
He loves his toys especially Dun-Dun the ted.
He always gets his head stuck in the holes he makes in the garden
So you see that's my dog Jack!

David Watkin (10)
Lightcliffe Preparatory School

SPIDER MONKEY

In the jungle eyes and ears
Peeking and hearing the chomping.
In the jungle see them jump
Tree to tree they never stop.
Tails and hands are all you see
While they're moving branch to branch.
All you hear is chomping and rustling.
Hear them howl, hear them munch, all the way through their dinner.
Smooth fur, rough fur, all around its body.
Its tail is like a question mark swinging through the trees.
Bananas, mangoes these lovely things to enjoy,
Kiwi, pineapple that's everything they can eat.
At night they sleep.
Their eyes go down, down and blank,
They're asleep. *Ssshhh!*

Lorna Butler (10)
Lightcliffe Preparatory School

SLOTH

Sloths are sluggish and slow
Climbing to tops of trees.
Smelly with algae growing in their hair.
Slothfully sleeping and swaying
Chomping plants and leaves.
Climbing higher and higher
With three toes clinging
To any branch, soon time to return to the
                            under-storey canopy.

Matthew Walton (10)
Lightcliffe Preparatory School

SLOTHS

In the humid heat of the day
They rest in the light of the sun.
Hungry, they slowly lumber and shuffle to find food.
They must be wary for they are prey.
Prey for cunning jaguar, nimble leopard or light ocelot.
They must keep a lookout and listen hard.
Hearing rainforest noises, they turn their solemn heads.
Their sleepy eyes searching around the understorey canopy.
Slowly they go to search for food
Juicy leaves, big, round, shiny berries
Slowly along the slippery liana which are swaying in the breeze
Slowly and steadily, slowly and steadily
Till they reach their destination.

Arabella Fox (11)
Lightcliffe Preparatory School

THE SPIDER MONKEYS' RACE

Swinging actively through the canopy
The spider monkeys race each other.
Their form of exercise is extremely good
Hey, he's gone past another!

It was true, the youngster who was certainly fit
Was catching up with the leader.
The competition between the two
Would have baffled the world's best reader.

They were now so close together
You could hardly see between.
The sun now made their coats so bright
As they were rather clean.

Finally when they'd got back home
Waiting for the others.
They sat there stuffing themselves with food
When along came their odd brothers.

David Wevill (10)
Lightcliffe Preparatory School

THE SPIDER MONKEY

The cheeky little spider monkey hops from branch to branch
With its cute little face and big cheeky smile.
With its huge, long tail hooking on chunky trees
Looking quite like a question mark, its body is the dot.
As it moves swiftly from branch to branch,
it chitter-chatters, chitter-chatters.
It has long slender limbs, which fly swiftly in the air.
With its big brown eyes, on its soft smooth face.
It peers into the depths of the jungle.

Jenny Wormald (10)
Lightcliffe Preparatory School

THE HARPY EAGLE

The harpy stood smart, cunning
With its powerful talons
Sinking into the helpless branch
Suddenly it spotted a little dark creature
Swinging tree to tree with its light body
The harpy took off with amazing speed
It dived like a trained skydiver
The poor creature lay dead.

William Edhouse (11)
Lightcliffe Preparatory School

SLOTH

A sloth, a sloth, whatever is a sloth?
With a face like a ferret and fear as deep as snow.
He has big strong arms
And a black and white back .
Oh sloth, oh sloth, where are you now?

Ben Taylor (10)
Lightcliffe Preparatory School

FIRST DAY AT THE SWIMMING BATHS

Getting off the bus
In through the doors
Smelling the chlorine
Changing into my swimming trunks
Having a nice warm shower
But it didn't last long
I walked along the edge of the pool
Then we got in
It was freezing cold
Half an hour of hard work
Finally we had to get out, I thought
But no, we had to dive in!
I sank to the bottom
But I swam back up and grabbed the edge of the pool
My goggles were on the floor of the pool
I had to swim to the bottom of the pool and get them
Getting out was awful
It was even colder than before
But the shower was hotter
Finally we got on the bus
When I got home my mum and dad were pleased.

Louis Sheridan (8)
Luddenden Dene J&I School

MY FIRST DAY AT SCHOOL

Walking through the gate
Waiting for the bell to ring
I felt quite nervous
Lots of children were around me
But then someone popped out
From behind me and said,
'Hi, what's your name?'
So I replied, 'It's Claire.'
The bell rang
We all lined up in three lines
We filed into lessons
At home time I knew I had a best friend
This was the best school year ever.

Claire Kneeshaw (8)
Luddenden Dene J&I School

MY BIRTHDAY EVE

My birthday is tomorrow
I cannot get to sleep
I am too excited
So down the stairs I creep.

Into the lounge
Where presents are lying there
Thinking of surprises
Behind the paper I will tear.

Now into the kitchen
Make sure no one's awake
Move everything out of the way
I'm sure that I can break.

Over in the corner
The fridge is awake
The humming gets louder
As I hunt for my cake.

'The cake's beautiful!' I whispered
'The best I've ever seen!'
It had stripy wax candles
And icing smooth and clean

I must have gone to bed
Because I think that I was dreaming
That I'd woken up to presents
Dressed in my party clothes gleaming.

Charlotte Gross (8)
Luddenden Dene J&I School

FIRST TIME

Goggles on, I am ready to jump in the six foot
Swimming the length, leg kicking, arms twirling.
On my front, am getting out
To walk back for another length.
Am getting in again, on my back
Am sinking, *ahh,* quick stomach up.
Time to get out.
We rush, shivering into the changing room.
Into the showers to get warm.
Getting dressed on the bus to go home.
It's the best day of the week!

Nicola Walker (9)
Luddenden Dene J&I School

Charging! Charging!

I was in a field when a bull came charging at me
My brother said, 'Run!'
I said, 'Run as fast as you can.'
I climbed over the fence and so did my brother.
The bull had a big snorting nose with a ring,
It had a face scarier than a ghost like a man in black.
It knocked me off the slippery fence.
I was very scared.
It was ramming its head into the fence.
I ran so fast I had to stop halfway
And I never returned to the field again.

Ryan Barrett (8)
Luddenden Dene J&I School

MY PET DOG

I got a new pet
He was full of energy
And he is cheeky.

He likes to play ball
His fur is soft and cuddly
He is lovely.

He is cute, I said
'I have had him for a while
Now he has cancer.'

Mum took him to the vets
He does not have that much energy
He is still going.

I feel sorry for him
He is only a young dog
I would hate to lose him.

Hannah Walker (9)
Luddenden Dene J&I School

MY BIRTHDAY

My ninth birthday
It was better than OK.
I got more than I dreamt of.
I didn't have a favourite present
I thought I was in Heaven for a second.
Sometimes I would get very small presents
But they were the best ones.
Some presents were late
But they were the really good ones
I couldn't imagine having a better day
Everything was great!
It was the best day of my life.

Leon Wadsworth (9)
Luddenden Dene J&I School

MY PET RAT JEREMY

My pet rat Jeremy
Lives in my room.
When I go to see him
He wriggles along my shoulder.
Then he runs down my arm onto my bed
He looks extremely happy.
Once he hid under my bedcover,
Finally he came out with a discarded sock.
Next he climbed on the pockets
He got wedged in one time, we rescued him.
Then I got him a milk drop
He ate it greedily.
Then he hid in his J-cloth.
I looked back it was Chloe my cat.
I shooed her off.

Billy Painter (9)
Luddenden Dene J&I School

FIRST DAY AT SCHOOL

On the first day of school
It was good.
But then I spilt my pop, on my top
I was mad,
And I got sad.
I cried.
And then it dried.
On the second day of school Mrs Bush
Said, 'Come on, Mush.'
I had a best friend called Sarah
We played together
We played on the bikes together
We painted together
And that was my friend Sarah for you.
I got done
It was not fun.

Natalie Hirst (9)
Luddenden Dene J&I School

FIRST TIME AT HALIFAX SWIMMING CLUB

Clothes off.
Lucky goggles on.
Shorts on.
In I go.
I'm holding my dad's hands real tight.
I'm jealous.
They're experts.
I'm having my assessment.
One length, front crawl.
Another length, breaststroke.
Half a length, backstroke.
I'm shivering.
Have I passed?
Have I not?
I've passed.
Extra spending money. Yes!

Thomas Lund (8)
Luddenden Dene J&I School

FIRST DAY

First day of school
Scared as a mouse.
People were chatting with their friends.
Everyone was big and I was small.
Felt like the missing link.
The bell rang, I was shocked.
What does assembly mean?
I was sat next to a stranger.
Listening to words I'd never heard.
Bell rang again, play time.
I was walking around lonely.
A strange girl came up to me,
I found out her name was Claire.
She held my hand,
I played with her,
Then we lined up.
The lesson carried on for like hours.
Play time, finally I was relieved.
I played with Claire again.
Because I knew that was her name now.
By the end of play time we were friends.
Now the lesson was colouring,
I did a picture for my mum.
Yeah, last play time,
Whoo hoo, I thought.
I played with Claire again.
She was really nice.
'Bring and Show time'
What does that mean?
Yeah, home time at last.
I was relieved to see my mum
She was relieved to see me
She was happy I'd had a good time.

Bethany Broadbent (8)
Luddenden Dene J&I School

FIRST FLIGHT

I heard I was going on holiday
I was really excited.
My grandma and auntie came down
They had to drive us to the airport
It was boring in the car.
Finally we got there, I turned from excitement to nerves.
As soon as we put any luggage on a trolley, we went inside the airport.
We lined up in the line going to Tenerife,
The wait was over, we came to the front of the queue.
My mum and dad put the suitcases on the conveyor,
It carried them to the plane.
After security and passport check,
We went into a room where they checked our bags.
We finally got through.
Time to board - one hour sitting on chairs watching planes.
We showed our passports to a man and walked past the box.
I was excited and a little bit nervous as soon as we got on the plane.
We found our seats and sat down.
I held my dad's hand.
We were taxiing around the corner,
We were facing the runway then we stopped.
I was asking my dad all sorts of questions why my plane had stopped.
Then the engine started running.
We set off, we went faster and faster in a straight line, and we were off.
My ears popped straight away.

Sadie Parkin (8)
Luddenden Dene J&I School

HIDDEN TREASURE

My teddy Lucy means everything to me
She sleeps with me to keep me company.
I will always love her.
I've had her since I was a baby
I have always loved her.
And she loves me.
I bring her downstairs every morning.
And she will always be my treasure.
She stays by my side until it is time for school.
She watches television with me.
And we have a little song
This is our song -
'I love you
You love me
We're a little family
I will love forever.
With a nick, knack paddy whack
I love you.'
She has shiny eyes
Very fluffy skin
And she keeps me warm every night
And we will always be a family
And I sing our song to get her to go to sleep.

Gemma Greenberry (8)
Luddenden Dene J&I School

HIDDEN TREASURE

One day I found a treasure from deep
In a big slippy sloppy seaweed heap.
There were jewels, gold and silver
That in the sea, shines and quivers.
I wanted to know where it came from
So I put a diving suit on.
And swam down deep
And landed in another heap.
I saw a sunken ship with holes in it
It looked like it had been bit.
I went inside the ship
Inside the ship it was a tip.
There were fish everywhere
They were over here and all over there.
A big shark was swimming through
Looking for something to chew.
It spotted me in a corner
And then I made a runner.
I slipped on a seaweed heap
And swam up from the deep.

Edward Whiteley (8)
Luddenden Dene J&I School

HIDDEN TREASURES

Hidden treasure are to me
My very important family.
Mum and Dad, brothers and sisters and my toy dog called Lucky.
More important than gold or silver
Diamond rings or bronze.
Without my family how my life would be empty.
No fun and games
No playing out
No joy into my life.
But with them it is great.

Lisa Wehden (8)
Luddenden Dene J&I School

FIRST TIME

Clothes off,
Shorts on,
Goggles on.
Get a shower,
Out of changing room,
Dash to diving board.
Starting to shiver.
The boy in front was up on the top board,
About to dive.
He dived,
He was like an expert,
He did a dive bomb.
I was so jealous.
So I shot to the top board,
It was my first time ever,
The water was a long way down.

Jon Galloway (8)
Luddenden Dene J&I School

VICTORY MATCH

I'm in the changing room
Pulling my socks up
Putting my shirt on
And my shorts
Players onto the pitch
The whistle has gone
The ball, clean and new
The crowd are cheering
There's a black shirt being pulled
The ref has sent off a player
The opposition manager is not pleased
It's half-time
Nice cold refreshments
You can see ten orange shirts
And eleven black shirts
The whistle goes
The ball is flying like a rocket
Ten minutes left
There goes the ball
The crowd cheer,
'There's a cracker!
Black shirts everywhere
Com on, we're 1-0 up
Keep it up lads!'
Ten seconds left
Finally the whistle goes
Both teams shake hands
My manager says,
'Victory
At last lads.'

Aaron John Alexander (8)
Luddenden Dene J&I School

MY HANDS

All day my hands are swaying, swooping and curling.
After the questions were over,
There would be a flapping noise of the books.
Then there would be a twitching sound of the pen lids.

At night they freeze and rest, the flapping noise stops,
So does the clicking and curling and swooping, everything's calm.

Jordan Haley (9)
Northowram J&I School

A CAUTIONARY TALE
(The story of Jason Rabbit who had an awful disgusting habit)

There was a boy called Jason Rabbit
Who had an awful disgusting habit
He sucked his smelly rotting toes
Till he was cleaned with a garden hose.
He screamed and screamed and screeched and screeched
Like a wimpy girl who had been bleached
With a boiling, burning toxic waste
And a full tube of toothy paste.
He went to the smelly, disgusting dump
For a great big scarlet hairy lump.
He stuffed them in his humongous mouth
The stuff went hurtling and tumbling south.
He got a terrible frightening illness
After he became very pilless.
He knew that he was definitely going to die
After he said 'I am the weakest link, goodbye!'

Danielle Graham (9)
Northowram J&I School

SOPHIE READ'S HABIT - A CAUTIONARY TALE
(The story of a girl who chewed her hair)

Sophie Read chewed her hair
and she needed special care.
She really couldn't get enough
of the horrible hairy stuff.
One day she chewed so much of her head
it was as long as pencil lead.

But then her hands became hairy
and she looked really scary.
She turned very round
all of a sudden she found . . .
She was a hair ball
and she let out a bad call.
She went home and was grumpy and meaner
so her mum sucked her up the vacuum cleaner.
Inside she sighed
and the following Wednesday she died.

Lydia Gibson (8)
Northowram J&I School

A CAUTIONARY TALE
(The story of Sophie Pear who wouldn't stop chewing her hair)

The worst habit of Sophie Pear
Was chewing her brown tatty hair.

The doctor came again to say
'You must stay in bed all day.'

Millions of nits came out of her mouth
They were all heading down south.

We all went to the lovely comfy bed
But in the morning Sophie's mum found she was dead.

Emily Godfrey (9)
Northowram J&I School

A CAUTIONARY TALE

Toby Greenhough
wouldn't stop eating flies
of course he died.

Toby had a bad disease
which did increase as he ate the fleas.

Toby said 'I love the beasts but I want them in a great big feast.'
It wouldn't surprise me if he died or of course ate a fly.

Toby ate one more fly and he started to die,
his tummy splat out and the gruesome things were out and about.

Toby Greenhough (8)
Northowram J&I School

BULLY

B ig, lashing, fat bully
U gly like a beast
L ittle spiky hairs on his head
L ittle rat ears
Y ou are a nasty ogre.

Rebecca Kitson (8)
Northowram J&I School

WINTER

Snow falls like rain drops
Fog is like moonlight smoothly
Sledging is a joy.

Robin Dance (9)
Northowram J&I School

BULLYING

B ullying all day kicking and punching
U sually staying up all night
L onely always spoiling games
L eft-out calling names
Y oung people he picks on, so you better beware.

Brittany Henderson (9)
Northowram J&I School

A CAUTIONARY TALE

The main bad habit of Joe Popper
He ate too much of a gobstopper.
The main bad habit of Joe Popper
He ate too much of a gobstopper.
His big red face went a different colour
If he ate anymore he would get fuller.
He felt a bit sick of his gobstopper ball
The doctor came, he was very tall.
The doctor said he was going to die
His mum and dad went off to cry.
On the day he passed away
All his family was in delay.

Ben Glennon (9)
Northowram J&I School

BULLY

B eginning to get angry
U nfriendly all day
L onely wanting a friend
L eft out in everything
Y elling at everyone.

Alexander Sugden (8)
Northowram J&I School

A CAUTIONARY TALE
(This is the tale of Pertunia Cleef who ground her life to a stop)

The main bad habit of Pertunia Cleef
Was grinding her brown and rotting teeth.
But what she did not understand
Is she might as well be eating sand.
After a few months her teeth got smaller
And her longing for hard food got a lot taller.
Soon she grew incredibly thin
She was nearly as thin as a drawing pin.
Her tummy started to grumble and moan
And her mouth rang just like a telephone.
One sunny day she started to cry
All of a sudden she happened to die.

Sophie Beverley (8)
Northowram J&I School

METAPHOR

All day they have different reactions to different objects.
When they grip, the tiny fingers haul, then abandon it gently.

But at night my hands swoop out feeling the fur of a teddy
as I fall into a deep slumber unaware of my actions.
A mystery to all until morning for the hands to start again.

Chloe Frances (9)
Northowram J&I School

THE STORY OF BENNY POPPER - A CAUTIONARY TALE

The main habit of Benny Popper was eating loads of gobstoppers.
He once was at the bowling alley, where he was on a winning tally.
Suddenly his belly split, his mother almost had a fit.
The stoppers rolled along the alley building on the winning tally.
The stoppers rolled and got a strike, a sickening pain just like a spike
On the floor was his head.
Benny Popper was surely dead.

Robert Brander (8)
Northowram J&I School

DAN THE MAN

Dan the man, big bad bully
His boots are big and his socks are woolly.

Dan the man is coming to town
You'd better watch out or he'll push you down.

Dan the man will kick and shout
He calls a name and he runs about.

Dan the man is really thick
Dan the man he makes you sick!

Gareth Moger & Daniel Murgatroyd (9)
Northowram J&I School

THE HYENA

I watched a big fat laughing hyena
Try to make for a champion pie-eater.

There was a bird inside the pie
Which then rose up into the sky.

The bird fell in its tormentor's mouth
Bird then went down that throat down south.

The hyena broke into a joke shop
It did a large and smelly plop.

It laughed and laughed and laughed out loud
In front of a large and smelly crowd.

Dear bird came out of the plot with a jump
He said 'Dear friend, you're very plump.'

A tiny mouse joined dear old bird,
Hyena thought it quite absurd.

He pounced on them in time for lunch,
He ate them both almost at once.

A reeking burp was what he needed
He tried with his might and he succeeded!

Freddy Vinehill-Cliffe (8)
Northowram J&I School

THE HANDS

All day long a beautiful tune comes out of the blue
$\qquad\qquad\qquad\qquad$ as they swoop at a pool.
They glide, they flutter all day long.
A squeaky noise turns into a tranquil melody.
But at night that melody fades as they lie still
$\qquad\qquad\qquad\qquad$ cuddled up till the light of dawn.

Hilary Dennett (8)
Northowram J&I School

BULLY

B   ig bad kicks
U   gly parched face
L   ashing out at people
L   inked with their friends
Y   oung strong boy.

Bradley Wilkinson (8)
Northowram J&I School

A CAUTIONARY TALE
(This is a story of a girl who kept eating toffee)

The main bad habit of Sarah Coffee
was eating yucky, sticky toffee.

Not only was it so, so bad
she ended up just like her dad.
Once her tummy had caught the horrid thing
she then heard her tummy do a ring.
Then she had a very bad ache,
Sarah called the doctor and he made her take
pills and yucky medicine to make her care,
and there she died on a knobbly stair.

Tara Taylor (9)
Northowram J&I School

A BULLY POEM

B ad person who hurts others
U pset because they have no friends.
L onely and neglected
L eft out and only has a teddy to cuddle
Y oung, but a lot older than the person they are bullying.

Victoria Newton (9)
Northowram J&I School

A CAUTIONARY TALE
(The tale of Gregory Sails who couldn't stop biting his nails)

The main bad habit of Gregory Sails
was all he did was bite his nails.
He did it on his small toes
he stuck his bad nails up his nose.
Until one day when he got really bad
his mother was proper mad.
She rang the doctor and he said
'He'll soon be the one around here dead.'
That dark night he went to bed
his nails are really small
they're as short as pencil lead.
The following day he was dead
just as the doctor had said.

Annie Smith (8)
Northowram J&I School

ACROSTIC

B   ullies frighten and thump and do horrible things like punch
they rip you and kick you.

U   nlike they are kind and nice to people and care for them.

L   ucky they don't come to my house to have a sleepover or wake
me up.

L   ucky I've got a friend who cares for me and looks after me when
I've fallen over.

Y   ucky people for fighting and kicking me. I'll tell the headmistress
and kill their bodies and tell them off forever.

Emma Unsworth (8)
Northowram J&I School

BULLY VICTIM

B   ullies are bad
U   nkind and nasty
L   ove picking on people
L   ike name calling
Y   our main enemy.

V   ery weak
I   nside they are scared
C   alled names
T   errified and sad
I   nside also upset
M   ad at the bully.

Sam Butterworth (9)
Northowram J&I School

WINTER HAIKU

Skidding icy roads
Snowflakes dropping to the ground
Gentle fire inside.

Tom Silson (9)
Northowram J&I School

BULLY

B   ig bad frown
U   gly and strong
L   aughing and bad
L   ashing hand
Y   oung and foolish.

Joel Gibson (9)
Northowram J&I School

A CAUTIONARY TALE
(The tale of Jordan Laces who pulled funny faces)

The main bad habit of Jordan Laces
Is that he always pulls funny faces.
He pulled some silly and some strange
Whatever the kind of range.
He pulled them hard, even harder
Even in his mother's larder.
But this was very, very strange
The wind had changed.
He didn't open his mouth
So he started to head south.
But half way there he started to die
Before he died he was going to be fried.

Suzie Lockey (9)
Northowram J&I School

MY BULLY

People pusher
Locker looker
Cat kicker
Dog hitter
Non crier
Children spier
Pen taker
Sadness maker.

Andrew Tordoff (8)
Northowram J&I School

NEWCASTLE UNITED

Award winner
Goal scorer
Net shaker
Corner taker
Ball winner
Football header
Ball passer
Goal scorer
Fan exciter
Long distance traveller
Team beater
Hard trainer
Money maker
Sunderland hater
Dream maker
Tynesider.

Daniel Phipps (10)
Northowram J&I School

ROLLER COASTER

Vertical suspender
Underground racer
Tummy turner
Head spinner
Sick producer
Fast thriller
Terror tower
Sudden stopper
Everlasting chugger
Ride rusher
Track inverter.

Richard Hoyle (11)
Northowram J&I School

Dog

People licker
Noise maker
Tail wagger
Bone muncher
Cat chaser
Frisbee catcher
Great runner
Loud barker
Lead puller
Tablecloth tugger.

Alexander Bales (11)
Northowram J&I School

SWEETS FAN

Gob stopper
Bubblegum popper
Sherbet dipper
Lollipop licker
Liquorice snapper
Candy cracker
Rock cruncher
Biscuit muncher
Tongue twister
Don't whisper!

Jonathan Lund (11)
Northowram J&I School

DENNIS THE MENACE

Pea shooter
Catapult firer
Softy hater
School skiver
Walter menacer
Pocket money decreaser
Water gun blaster
Sweet scoffer
Dog lover
Bath avoider
Slipper hit taker.

Joshua Thwaites (11)
Northowram J&I School

BABY

Noisy screamer
Mess maker
Dirty spitter
Rattle shaker
Bad crawler
Bottom faller
Milk drinker
Little fiddler
Nose picker
Bogie flicker
Smell producer
Nappy filler
Cling on cuddler
Silent sleeper
Juice drinker
Food splatterer
Hair puller
Cute looker
Cheeky grinner.

Brooke Hanks (11)
Northowram J&I School

TEENAGER

Eyebrow plucker
Lipstick wearer
Nail painter
Night-time clubber
Lad chaser
Poster kisser
Spot picker
Mum tormentor
Trend setter
Mobile chatterer
Hair curler
Skin toner
Music blaster
New shoes rub her
All time shopper
Eyelash flutterer
Boyfriend ditcher.

Sarah McTier (11)
Northowram J&I School

HAND

Pen writer
Horn honker
Book flicker
Nose picker
Light twitcher
Earring fiddler
Cup holder
Animal stroker
Tissue puller
Curtain tugger
Toilet flusher.

Nicola Stanley (11)
Northowram J&I School

MY SISTER

Bathroom hogger
Room messer
Night raker
Hair fiddler
Music listener
Boyfriend kisser
Dad arguer
Great shopper
Netball lover
Pub worker
Gym trainer
Trend setter
The best clubber
Homework loser
Phone user
Friend stealer
Drinks Tequila
Make-up borrower
The best ever.

Katie Walton (11)
Northowram J&I School

DOG

Bark maker
Stick chaser
Food gobbler
Fire sleeper
Fur moulter
King walker
Food beggar
Sun bather
River swimmer
Slipper hider
Lonely crier
Toast lover
Owner greeter.

Siân Farr (11)
Northowram J&I School

MOUSE

Cheese eater
Cat attractor
Speedy scuttler
Mess maker
Sneaky stealer
Cat hider
Fur frightener
Wall tapper
Wire biter
High pitched squeaker
Stringy tail.

Emily Upite (11)
Northowram J&I School

TODDLER

Cute looker
Cheeky smiler
Face scratcher
Recent walker
Milk moaner
Speak starter
Sweet wanter
Dummy sucker
Bed wetter
Toy chewer
Teeth grower
Food slopper
Noisy chuckler
Paper tearer
Rattle shaker
Nosey parker.

Joanne Mount (10)
Northowram J&I School

TEENAGER

Boy kisser
Class misser
Make-up whopper
Party popper
Lipstick lover
Bossy mother
Baby sitter
Girl hitter
Night clubber
Big brother
Boy dater
Mate befriender.

Emma Galvin (10)
Northowram J&I School

TEACHERS

Finger pointer
Word changer
Blackboard writer
Trouble sighter
Book marker
Story teller
Child helper
Letter composer
Homework setter
Model maker
Work receiver
Example shower
Sum adder
Playground watcher
Cloakroom cleaner.

Laura Dance (10)
Northowram J&I School

JAMES BOND

Woman catcher
Gun snatcher
Baddy stopper
Champagne popper
Qteaser
Government pleaser
Terrorist killer
Drink swiler
Gadget user
A real bruiser
Head breaker
Cocktail shaker
Mad driver
Deep-sea diver
In Heaven
It's 007.

Liam Riding (10)
Northowram J&I School

SNOW

White sprinkler
Field coverer
Snowball maker
Fence topper
Car freezer
World whitener
Water solidifier
Car slider
Snowman maker
School closer
Children exciter.

Jade Upite (10)
Northowram J&I School

LIFEGUARD

Lifesaver
Sun bather
Boat rider
Sea diver
Ocean swimmer
Medal winner
Hard trainer
Woman gazer
Muscle bulger
Fashion sculpture
Sand trader
Body builder
Shore starer
Uniform wearer
Beach survivor
Patrol driver.

Charlotte Clee (10)
Northowram J&I School

RAIN

People soaker
Leaf puller
Puddle maker
Gutter filler
Black cloud constructor
Umbrella raiser
Rainbow producer
Coat soaker
Drip dripper
Face frowner
Hair wetter
Ground flooder.

Bethany Bowers (10)
Northowram J&I School

TEENAGER

Door banging
Shoe wanging
Spot popping
Clothes shopping
Nail painting
Boy dating
Lipstick wearing
Make-up sharing
Dancing diva
Best friend leaver
Night clubbing
Always pubbing
Homework forgetting
Room messing
Music lover
Under cover.

Teenager!

Nadia Al-Chalaby (10)
Northowram J&I School

RABBIT

Grass eater
Swede scoffer
Mess maker
People biter
Dad scratcher
Carrot adorer
High hopper
Water sipper
Wood muncher
Cage wrecker
Great observer
Lettuce stealer
Burrow digger
Whisker twitcher
Night feeder.

Ben Warrington (10)
Northowram J&I School

A DOG

Basket heater
Food eater
Cat chaser
Moon racer
Sleep curler
Grass grower
Tree wetter
Paper ripper
Owner puller
Head tilter
Ear perker
Tail twirler
Loud barker
Human lover
House stinker.

Henry Naylor (10)
Northowram J&I School

FIRE

Wood burner
Smoke blower
Heat giver
Spark spitter
In the dark glower
Flame shiner
Woods destroyer
Life threatener
Food cooker
Water boiler
Plastic melter
Metal bender.

Michael Hoyle (10)
Northowram J&I School

STORM

Puddle maker
Home destroyer
Reservoir filler
Drum rumbler
Fence knocker
Animal scarer
Tree swayer
House rattler
Paper blower.

Jake Glennon (10)
Northowram J&I School

TEENAGER

Window smasher
Head basher
Alleyway lurker
Beer burper
Tobacco smoker
Kid choker
Rule breaker
Drug taker
Stud wearer
Chain bearer
Heavy metal listener
Girl kisser.

Richard Cole (10)
Northowram J&I School

GRANDMA

Jumper knitter
Baby sitter
Treat giver
Flour siever
Cake baker
Jigsaw maker
Fussy helper
Polite chelper
Glasses wearer
Plant carer
Homework interferer
Moving nearer
Aggh Gran!

Thomas Gott (10)
Northowram J&I School

FIRE

Cold shelter
Snow melter
Spark shooter
Smoke producer
House heater
Night warmer
Firework lighter
Wax melter
Paper churner
Colour displayer
Emergency creator
Water evaporator.

Thomas Holdsworth (10)
Northowram J&I School

WHEN I LOST MY BROTHER

When I lost my brother
It was awfully quiet and sad
My mum kept on crying for hours on end
Saying she was alright but I knew she wasn't.

When I lost my brother
All his things were thrown away
His crib, his favourite teddy, were all put in the skip
My mum said 'You're the only child now.'

When I lost my brother
Everything changed
My mum, me, my grandma, grandad, uncle and aunt
But now we remember the good times we had
When my brother was still here and everyone was glad.

Naomi Li (10)
St Malachy's Primary School, Illingworth

RAIN

As the rain falls down
It clatters against the ground
In the rivers it gets deep
You can hear it when you sleep
Rain, rain go away.

Sometimes the rain
Dances in pain
As it begins to fall
It makes ripples on the puddle wall
Rain, rain go away.

As the rain fills up the clouds
After a moment it hits the ground.

After hours it gets hot
No more water
Comes from the taps
Rain, rain come back.

Abigail Lord (11)
St Malachy's Primary School, Illingworth

THE BULLIES

The bullies are round the corner
What am I going to do?
Maybe I'll just hide
They won't have a clue.

The bullies are round the corner
Planning their next move
Taunting and name calling
Do they have something to prove?

The bullies are round the corner
Oh no, they've got quite near
I'm starting to get worried
I've started to sweat for fear.

The bullies are round the corner
No they aren't, they've gone
Have they crept up behind me?
No, not even one.

The bullies aren't round the corner
What a big relief
Now I can walk home
In silence and in peace.

Coral Byrne (11)
St Malachy's Primary School, Illingworth

THE BEACH

Long, long ago in a near enough land
Where I used to visit
Where blue was the sea and gold was the sand
And the wind blew gently.

The stones and pebbles lay on the ground
And I just sat and watched them
Not even making the slightest sound
All shapes and sizes, just gems.

The seaweed scatters about in the water
But didn't move out of place
There came shoal's mother, father and daughter
With stripes on their fins like painted zebras.

I didn't want to leave that place
I really wanted to stay
I didn't care if I was alone
I'd do anything to watch the sea gently sway.

Kirsty McCormack (10)
St Malachy's Primary School, Illingworth

SNOW

Snow is like
A pale face covering up the sky.
Snow is like
An extended sheet on the bed of the world.
Snow is like
A piece of paper waiting to receive my poem.
Snow is like
A cream bun overflowing from the edges of a dish.
Snow is
Something I love!

Louise Royston (9)
St Malachy's Primary School, Illingworth

THE WIND

The wind
howls
like a werewolf at the strike of midnight.
The wind
roars
like a hungry lion waiting for its prey.
The wind
damages
like a volcano after it's erupted.
The wind
sings
like a bird practising its dawn chorus.
The wind
blows
like a child blowing out candles on the birthday cake.
The wind
smashes
like children hurling stones in at someone's window.
The wind
huffs
like the wolf from the three little pigs.
The wind
crashes
like two cars bashing together.

Kirsty Whitworth (10)
St Malachy's Primary School, Illingworth

THE MATCH

The coach pulled up outside the ground
Knowing we were gonna lose
Across the road, the local pub
Inside people drinking booze.

We all got changed into our strip
Numbers one to eleven.
The clock on the wall told the time
It showed a quarter to seven.

We slowly walked out into the tunnel
The walls all plain and white
Opposite me, numbers two and seven
Nearly got into a fight.

We saw the field and the goals
We felt the soft wet grass
Nine players stood around a ball
Eight shouting 'Gimme a pass.'

We took the kick-off and got the ball forward
It landed in front of their man.
Our player went in with a flying tackle
He earned a red card and a one match ban.

The half-time whistle finally blew
We were lucky not to concede
They were also so unlucky!
Not to be in the lead.

The rest of the game went quickly enough
The full-time whistle blew
In this match we'd lost but scored
And scoring is something new!

Craig Wilson (10)
St Malachy's Primary School, Illingworth

SNOW

Snow is
thick white chalk writing on a
blackboard telling children what to do.

Snow is
clouds floating through an ice-cold
blue sky on their way to another country.

Snow is
newly printed paper waiting to be
written on.

Snow is
an angel on its way down from
Heaven to send a message from God.

Snow is
a soft bed ready for someone
to sink into.

Snow is
a sheet blowing on a washing
line in the middle of spring.

Snow is
gentle like a mother to her baby.

Hannah Alderson (10)
St Malachy's Primary School, Illingworth

THE MOON!

The moon
spins
like a fairground wheel lighting up towards the top.

The moon
floats
like a duck on still water.

The moon
glows
like a candle burning in the night.

The moon
sparkles
like a diamond on a precious ring.

The moon
overlooks
the world like a bird in the sky.

Rachael Basett (11)
St Malachy's Primary School, Illingworth

HAPPINESS IS

Happiness is
Something that you enjoy and like to do.

Happiness
Means you're in a good mood and you're ready to explode in delight.

Happiness is
Joy and love to each other.

Happiness is
Food for the poor and winning for champions.

Happiness is
A person's future waiting to appear

Happiness is
A child's favourite toy and an adult job.

Kyle Tyers (11)
St Malachy's Primary School, Illingworth

CATS' EYES

Cats' eyes
glow
Like
Illuminous lights in the dark.

Cats' eyes are
round
balls staring at its owner.

Cats' eyes glare
like
lions looking for prey.

Cats' eyes are
green
grass on the fields.

Cats' eyes
sink
in their sockets like bones in soft mud.

Cats' eyes
look
at me before I go to bed!

Krystle Walker (9)
St Malachy's Primary School, Illingworth

THE WIND

The wind
Is an angry man ready to lash out.

The wind
Is a whimpering dog waiting to play.

The wind
Is a happy girl singing in the night.

The wind
Is a fierce lion ready to kill.

The wind
Is a boy sitting on a wall crying.

The wind
Is a baby rattling its toys.

Emma Louise Smith (11)
St Malachy's Primary School, Illingworth

BOB

He goes around the street at night
But nobody can see him
He is a very lonely man
I wouldn't want to be him
He is the ghost of Bob.

He can sneak in people's homes
As quiet as a mouse
It's good no one can see him
Staring from their house
That mean old ghost of Bob.

He's a thief, he's a crook
He isn't very kind
He cannot harm the living
He won't creep up from behind
He is the ghost of Bob.

He would like to go up there
So he could take a rest
But all the angels think
He's a nuisance like the rest
The selfish ghost of Bob.

Aaron Stephenson (11)
St Malachy's Primary School, Illingworth

THE SNOW

The snow
Clings
Like a cat's claw sticking to your clothes.

The snow
Falls
Like water tumbling down a mountain.

The snow
Floats
Like the white clouds in the light blue sky.

The snow melts
Like ice cream on a hot sunny day.

The snow
Carpets the ground
Like a big white rug in my living room.

Jessica Pollard (10)
St Malachy's Primary School, Illingworth

BLUE

Blue is
A cloudless sky
Suspended over the Earth.

Blue is
A colour
Of night and day.

Blue is
A residence
For sealife.

Blue is
A splash of paint
On and above the Earth.

Blue is
A face
Panting for breath.

Gabrielle Riding (9)
St Malachy's Primary School, Illingworth

SADNESS IS . . .

Sadness is like a grey, dull sky floating in thin air.
Sadness is like a baby crying and shouting in despair.
Sadness is like a flower slowly rotting away.
Sadness is a tragedy which has happened that very day.
Sadness is like a balloon being popped with a very sharp pin.
Sadness is like a treasured toy thrown away in the bin.
Sadness is a feeling that you always fear.
Sadness is a feeling that no one else can hear.

Niall Brady (11)
St Malachy's Primary School, Illingworth

MY BOX

What am I able to build with my box?
Houses and trains, rockets and shops
I'll use the big boxes in my room
So I can fly to the moon.

The floor is the launch-pad, the bed is the moon
I'll get ready for take-off and await my doom
The man comes up to me telling what's right
To make sure that I'm able to fly tonight.

I jump in my rocket to go sky high
I look out the window and wave goodbye
I look at my teddy and start to cry
I do not want to say goodbye.

Shannon Southall (10)
St Malachy's Primary School, Illingworth

GHOSTS

Drifting through the dead of night
Don't go out they'll give you a fright
It is a blank cover in the sky
Floating very, very high.
It is a cloud waiting to scare
It'll give you a warning *please take care.*
So don't go out at the dead of night
Only go out when it's light.

Brittany Gaukroger (10)
St Malachy's Primary School, Illingworth

THE SUN

The sun is like a bright yellow sphere and like a
Strong ball of sand.
The sun is like a shiny ball of fire and like a
Strong planet.
The sun is like a very hot sphere.
The sun is like a big orange on fire, with juice pouring out of it.
The sun is like a volcano in the dark sky.

Joshua Crabtree (10)
St Malachy's Primary School, Illingworth

THE MOON

The moon is
An eye looking at you in the dark.
Like a glowing biscuit waiting to be eaten
From the sky.
Like a block of glistening white cheese
With a silver ring round it.
Like a ghostly smile trying to get you out of space.
Like a ghost hiding in the sky as people watch.
Like a kite dancing around in the midsummer night.

Emma Guy (10)
St Malachy's Primary School, Illingworth

SKIPPING ROPE SONG

St Malachy's is the best,
Deanfield is a pest.
They took our field,
So they can play.
We watch through the railings,
Every day.
Jump up and down,
Because you see
We've a new field.
Wow yippee!

Lindsay Royston (11)
St Malachy's Primary School, Illingworth

THE CRIME FIGHTER'S DOG

There was a boy who had a dog as fat as a pig
That was because he liked eating loads of figs
But the crime fighter was planning on having a jig
The dog just pulled off the fighter's mum's wig,
Old dog as fat as a hog.
They went into town to fight some crime
But the big fat dog had to do a mime
Then the dog got a great big lime
The crime fighter's dog.

Then seeing some crime they went off, the dog went to hide
'Let's fight some crime' the crime fighter cried
He leapt at the criminal but he missed so wide
The criminal then getting away he tried.
Then came down hitting the criminal was a big tall log
It was the dog that had pushed it down
The store manager gave him a crown
The criminal just gave a frown
The crime fighter's dog.

Along came the police to take him away
There on the floor he just lay
'Stand up please' the policeman did say
Into the van he went landing on some hay
They drove away in the fog.
The dog and the fighter went down the street hop, hop, hop
On the way they stopped for some pop
At the big hypermarket shop
The crime fighter's dog.

They got home it was all black
For the white paint they did lack
The dog went and got in his sack
But then started itching his back.
Dreaming of going for a jog
He went to the beach and got bit by a crab,
Then off to the professor's lab
Going home he got in a cab
The crime fighter's dog.

Jack Viney (10)
St Malachy's Primary School, Illingworth

THE SUN

The sun is
Like a big orange on fire, with juice pouring out of it.
The sun is
Like a football getting kicked around the solar system.
The sun is
Like an erupted volcano in the dark sky.
The sun is
Like a leech sucking up the water from the Earth.
The sun is
Like a big hot air balloon on fire.

Michael Long (10)
St Malachy's Primary School, Illingworth

MY FAMILY, MY TREASURE

My treasure is my family.
They are like an unstopping merry-go-round always caring.
They are like the water surrounding an island,
Their love surrounding me.
They are like gold, a treasure within.
They are like a miracle, sharing good news and bad.
They are like a treasure hunt only easy to find.
They are my family and I'm so grateful for that.

Sinéad Devlin (11)
St Malachy's Primary School, Illingworth

THE MOON IS . . .

Like a glowing pearl that
Glistens through the night.

Like an eye that watches you
From up above.

Like a white button swirling
Round in the sky.

Like a sparkly ghost that
Lightens up the world.

Like a shiny smile when
It's out shining.

Like a biscuit waiting
To be eaten.

Victoria Rye (11)
St Malachy's Primary School, Illingworth

THE MYSTERIOUS PLANET

The mysterious planet is like a needle in a haystack.
The mysterious planet is like a grain of sand in the desert.
The mysterious planet is like dust in an attic
The mysterious planet Is lost like a star in space.

Joe O'Byrne (11)
St Malachy's Primary School, Illingworth

HIDDEN TREASURE

Hidden treasure is like a casket of sparkling gold.
Hidden treasure is like a lonely box stranded on the bottom
                                                    of the ocean.
Hidden treasure is like a star that has fallen from the sky.
Hidden treasure is like a sour lemon waiting hopelessly to be found.
Hidden treasure is like a heart with our precious things inside.

Jenny Robertshaw (11)
St Malachy's Primary School, Illingworth

SISTERS

Sisters are like a stinging pain
That won't go away.

Sisters are like an alien in disguise
That as soon as it gets you, you have no chance of escape.

Sisters are like giant insects
That try to suck up to you.

Sisters are like curly hair robots
That does the same things over and over again.

Sisters, are they really that bad?
Actually it's my sisters that think I'm mad.

Stephen Walker (11)
St Malachy's Primary School, Illingworth

TEACHERS

A teacher is like a fire breathing
Dragoon a Monday morning.

A head teacher is like a thin lamp post
That no one wants to turn on.

A supply teacher is like a monster who
Tells you to read.

A teacher is like a crab nipping you
If you do wrong times tables.

A head teacher is like a candle that
Needs to be put out.

A teacher is like a motor bike racing
Down when you talk or out of line.

Sarah Newburn (10)
St Malachy's Primary School, Illingworth

MY TREASURE

Treasure is
personal things that are special to you.
Treasure is
like a part of you, you don't want to give away.
Treasure is
like a lifetime of memories only you know about.
Treasure is
like a box of gold that you don't want to give away.
Treasure is
like a heart full of dreams
Treasure is
love from others.

Margaret Theresa Spellman (10)
St Malachy's Primary School, Illingworth

THE MOON

The moon is like a face of
glitter up in the nights sky.

Like a glistening, silver pearly up above.

Like a glowing eye saying 'Hello.'

It's like a sparkling bubble
half or whole.

It's like a ghostly button.

It's like a man in the sky.

Lauren Taylor (10)
St Malachy's Primary School, Illingworth

TREASURE

Treasure is the hand holding all the golden rings.
Treasure is the big box in the sea full of good goodies.
Treasure is the goal for the pirates to find the jewellery.
Treasure is the till which contains gold, silver and pearls.
Treasure is the mystery which has to be solved with a shovel and map.

Joshua Magro (10)
St Malachy's Primary School, Illingworth

THE NIGHT

The night is a black sheet covering the sky.
The night is a face that says bye-bye.
The night is a silent night whispering by its self.
The night is a black shining armour fighting in silence.
The night is a black sheet with glitter that are stars covering the sky.

Samantha Egan (10)
St Malachy's Primary School, Illingworth

THE ALIENS

The aliens are like us
But with a lot less fuss.

The aliens are like us
But taller than a bus.

The aliens are like us
But we don't like to discuss it.

To them we are the aliens
We're from Earth
And they're from Mars.

Christopher Turver (9)
St Malachy's Primary School, Illingworth

THE GARDEN

The garden is like a kingdom of wisdom
The garden is like a powerful king
The garden is like a freshly peeled apple
The garden is like a home-made pie
The garden is like a plump tree waiting for someone to take a bite
The garden is everything you wished for.

Kirsty O'Halloran (10)
St Malachy's Primary School, Illingworth

SKY

The sky is blue dye hovering in mid-air.
The sky is an inverted ocean with white swans floating silently in it.
The sky is a turquoise ceiling with cream paint splattered on it
The sky is smoke from a wild fire rising higher into the atmosphere
The sky is perfection for me.

Bradley Holroyd (10)
St Malachy's Primary School, Illingworth

MY FEAR

I'm afraid of the dark
Terrified, frightening dark
Even the word *darkness* scares me
Just seeing pitch-black, nothing, loneliness
It's like it's going to punch me
Hearing the clock ticking, tick-tock, tick-tock
The wind outside howling, shouting 'I want to come in.'
Seeing nothing
Being on my own in my bedroom
Being with no one
Loneliness, horrible feeling, terrifying
Making long shadows
The crack in the door looks like a mouth saying
'You're on your own,' and the evil laughter ringing in my head
Snuggling up in my cold, cold bed
My face goes white like a ghost
A tree tapping on the window
What is that . . .? Nothing.
A fox crying like a screaming baby
Ooooo, I think I'm going to scream myself.
But I keep myself as quiet as a mouse in my cold, cold bed
Helpless, all I have to do is wait till morning
But I don't think morning would come in this cold, dark place
Crying I can't do anything
Darkness kills!
Cold, dark scary -
Terrified, horrified, petrified -
Rooted to the spot
Darkness! The most frightening word in the world
That is my fear!

Emily Horton (9)
Salterlee Primary School

SHEEP DOG

Sheep are best to chase.
Herding them comes naturally to me.
Easy-peasy, one good bark does the trick.
Even when it goes wrong somehow I look good.
Pens are for tidying up sheep. When I hear the gate go click
I know I'm boss.
Dodging in and out of the herd, I feel fast and free.
Oh, how clever I am.
Good times come from chasing sheep
That's why I enjoy my work so much.

Hannah Bodrozic (10)
Salterlee Primary School

MY FAMILY

I have a sister she is not very nice
I have a mum she's had children twice
I had a dad who adores rice
I have a brother who has pet mice
I have a dog who had lice
That is my family, it's not very nice
But I love them all very much.

Charlotte Lines (10)
Salterlee Primary School

ANIMALS

Pigs are fat
Pigs are smelly
Pigs eat too much so they have a fat belly.

Cats and dogs are very strange
They chase each other
They never change.

I have a mouse in my room
It likes to sleep
And hide under the broom.

Daniel Greenwood (11)
Salterlee Primary School

THE DEMON TEDDY

The teddy is a cuddly toy
But at night it comes alive
And does such naughty things
It climbs about and jumps and shouts
But in the morning when you stop snoring
It's back beside you still and smiling.

Freya Thoseby (9)
Salterlee Primary School

TEDDY BEARS

Teddy bears are silky and warm
You cuddle them all night
Some are brown, some are silver
Some are even black and white
You give them cute and lovely names
Such as Harry or Barney
Teddy bears can be big, they even can be small
Teddy bears are my favourite things - ever!
I love them so much,
I can't help to touch any that I see.
Because I love teddy bears.

Francesca Bland (9)
Salterlee Primary School

THE WIND

The wind blows and howls all the time
in that bedroom of mine.
The wind is so powerful the dirt
goes into your eyes.
And see the storm in the sky
The wind is very wild
and suddenly it goes very mild.
Then very, very, very fast!
It seems to have a mind of
its own.

Amy Duckett (9)
Salterlee Primary School

SNOW

When you walk on snow
The sound is *crunch, crunch, crunch.*

Snow is good for having fun
But it melts when it's in the sun.

Making snowmen, it is great
But if you are just too late
Down, down they tumble and all too soon they have disappeared.

Christian Georgiou (10)
Salterlee Primary School

CATS

Cats are soft and furry
They chase their tails all around the room
They screech at mail coming through the door
They go on walks, even though they can't talk
They hide in hats, they fight with other cats
Sometimes they hide under mats.
You will never catch them they will go too fast
If you ever get one you will see what I mean
You get them old or young, it does not matter, they're only cats.

Niall Smith (9)
Salterlee Primary School

THE WIND

The wind can be strong and powerful
The wind can be nice and calm
The wind can be wild
The wind blows like a wolf howling
The wind can be hot or cold like me and you
Nobody can stop it.

Danielle Stephenson (10)
Salterlee Primary School

THE WAY DOWN THE VALLEY

The autumn leaves on the autumn trees
Gathering around as we go
Into a deep, deep wood
Lower, lower low.

A little stream runs by
Never stopping, always running
Across a little bridge and up
A muddy track
And back to Salterlee School.

Danielle Cotton (10)
Salterlee Primary School

THE VALLEY

V alley is a wonderful place to be
A ll the trees and all the birds you can see.
L ovely woods and beautiful scenes
L ove to cross the glittering streams.
E xciting paths where you don't know where you are
Y elling out for more and more.

Natasha O'Hara (11)
Salterlee Primary School

APPLES

Like a sick face
Or a red world
The flying, buzzing creatures come
As the summer rain falls on the small planets
And the apples grow and grow and grow
Until they fall
Onto the ever waiting grass
Where they lie - waiting for teeth
To sink into their rotting flesh
And the old tree waits -
For autumn -
To fall again.

Calum Smith (10)
Salterlee Primary School

WASPS

Wasps do a lot of pestering, pestering and stinging, stinging
It really, really hurts
They fly up out of the flowers and it's really, really scary
I wish, I wish, I wish
They didn't swoop up on you when you're not looking1

Isobel Mears-Sykes (8)
Wainstalls J&I School

SNAKES

Slimy sticky snakes go *ssss*
Slipping whirling snakes go *ssss*
Sticky slimy snakes eating animals
Snakes go *ssss*
I hate snakes.

Lynsie Link (8)
Wainstalls J&I School

DON'T CLIMB WALLS

George Falls can't help climbing walls.
George Falls gets stuck and cries and calls.
The next day he died the same way.
In 1920 the 31st day of May.
So don't try climbing walls my boys
Just sit and play with your toys.

Holly Beaumont (9)
Wainstalls J&I School

THE LADY OF SHALOTT

'Oh Lancelot, help me, I pray
I may not live another day
Help me from this tower grey
On the cold hard floor on which I lay
Help me down to Camelot
An unknown curse is put upon me
Take me through the willow trees
To the people who are curse free.'
Cried the Lady of Shalott

Sir Lancelot reacted quick
'I hear a women who seems to be sick
Who's trapped inside by stone and brick
Of a castle grey and majestic.'
Said the brave knight Lancelot.
He rescued her within two minutes
A beautiful wife he did inherit
The curse just made the mirror split
As they lived happily in Camelot.

Joshua Ward (10)
Wainstalls J&I School

THE GIRL WHO WAS FAT AND CHUBBY

Jessica was a fat chubby child
She was very, very, very spoiled
She screamed going upstairs at ten
Then she started throwing her chess men
Then she hit the wall and hit her head
And then they found out that she was dead!

Daniel Futerko (8)
Wainstalls J&I School

MARTIN BROWN

Martin Brown was very greedy.
He was certainly not weedy.
In a small doorway he got stuck
His next door neighbours came to look
In his stomach he felt a pang
Then he exploded with a *bang*.

Stacey Link (9)
Wainstalls J&I School

BONFIRE NIGHT

Here we all are shivering in the cold
All the toffee apples have been sold
The fire being just brightly shining
My brother is whining
The fire is beaming
The fire engine is screaming
Here we all are shivering in the cold
All the toffee apples have been sold.

Sophie Smith (10)
Wainstalls J&I School

SNAKES

I hate snakes
Slippery wriggly
Forked tongues sticking out at me
Dangerous poisonous
Fast scary
The way it hisses at me
Frightening
Fast movers
Slithery long tongues
Oh no
It's heading for me!

Olivia Sutcliffe (8)
Wainstalls J&I School

ON HALLOWE'EN NIGHT

On Hallowe'en night
At the disco in Wainny
People wanted to give you a scare.

Their spooky costumes
Their ugly faces
They wore to give people a really big fright.

Lots of kids went out that night
Came knocking on my door
Knock! Knock!
What's that?

Bats' eyes gleaming like diamonds
Swooping from house to house
I am at the disco
I open the door
I scream, *'Arraacchh!'*

Jess Lumb (8)
Wainstalls J&I School

WASPS

Buzz, buzz
Wasps sting
Wasps sting
Mischievous wasps pester me
Irritating pests
Yellow and black ones
Ahh, they fly out at me
Oval shaped wasps
Bulgy is the wrong word
Skinny wasps
I hate wasps!

Sophie Hoyle (8)
Wainstalls J&I School

SNAKES

Slippery venom biting snake
Snake!
Eating animals whole
I hate snakes!
Sticky and stupid manners
I don't like snakes!
Hissing sliding *ssss*
I hate snakes
They are scary and creepy
Snakes, snakes!
Snakes make me jump
I don't like snakes!
Hissing and sliding snakes.

Thomas Thorp (8)
Wainstalls J&I School

BEES

I hate bees
Buzzing and buzzing
Flying near you
Trying to get them away
Buzzing and buzzing
The next thing you know
Sting!
It hurts
Buzzing and buzzing
Flying near you.

Xavier St Hilaire-Knowles (8)
Wainstalls J&I School

FLORENCE FREDRICA HAILS

Florence Fredrica Hails
Liked biting her sharp nails
At last she swallowed her last one
And now her nails are all gone
She got snuggled up in bed
In the morning she will be dead.

Gemma Dyson (10)
Wainstalls J&I School

BONFIRE NIGHT

I see sparklers sparkling in the air
Everybody holding them, just like they don't care.
Sparklers going, going, gone.
Black smoke everywhere, people coughing, people even choking.
Burning pies and mushy peas smell in the air.
Hot dogs sizzling in the pan.
Stinking of smoke all around the garden.
Parking on a tray, ready to be served.
Let's get ready, the fire begins and everybody sings.

Ben Wilby (9)
Wainstalls J&I School

LIZARDS

Lizards make me scream
Making me feel sick
Lizards make me scream
Slippy and sliding
Lizards make me scream
Moves quickly and shuffles away
Lizards make me scream
Skinny body
Lizards make me scream
Running away from you
Lizards make me run away
Camouflaged in green forests
Horrid lizards!

Natalie Carter (8)
Wainstalls J&I School

CRABS

Crabs are horrible
I hate the way
The crab sneaks up on you
I hate the quick pinch
The crab gives you
The colour is terrible
Orange and black
I hate it
Walking sideways
I hate it really
I hate crabs
I really do
I hate the crabs clapping claws
Making such a sound
Tiny red eyes
Blinking at me
I hate crabs
I really do
Lying still ready to pounce.

Hannah Moran (8)
Wainstalls J&I School